How to Be Hopeful, Joyful, and Peaceful

Bee Devotionals By Sheila Textor

Copyright © 2025 by Sheila Textor, Bee Ministries.
All rights reserved. No part of this book may be reproduced, transmitted, or distributed in any form or by electronic means without prior written permission of the publisher, except in the form of short quotations for book reviews and certain other noncommercial uses permitted by copyright law.

Independently published by Bee Ministries.
Manila, Arkansas

ISBN: 979-8-9887297-3-0

All scriptures used in this devotional come from the King James Version of the Bible, which exists in the public domain in the United States.

Interior art designed for Bee Ministries by Victoria Neal @victorianeal2001.

Check out Sheila's other works on Amazon:
Life After the Mistake
How to Bee Prosperous
How to Be Intentional With Your Words
How to Be Healthy, Wealthy, and Wise
How to Be Prayerful, Powerful, and Purposeful
How to Believe in Your Dreams
ebook: *How to Be a Writer*

Find Sheila on YouTube at Bee Ministries
Facebook @LifeAfterTheMistake

How to Be Hopeful, Joyful, and Peacful

By Sheila Textor

Contents

PART 1

Introduction 6
Day 1 8
Day 2 12
Day 3 16
Day 4 20
Day 5 24
Day 6 28
Day 7 32
Day 8 36
Day 9 40
Day 10 44

PART 2

Day 11 50
Day 12 54
Day 13 58
Day 14 62
Day 15 66
Day 16 70
Day 17 74
Day 18 78
Day 19 82
Day 20 86

PART 3

Day 21 92
Day 22 96
Day 23 100
Day 24 104
Day 25 108
Day 26 112
Day 27 116
Day 28 120
Day 29 124
Day 30 128
Day 31 132

Why bees? 136

Introduction

We all need hope, joy, and peace in times of uncertainty. These three staples are a must in the Christian's walk. Do we always have them? No, sometimes we forfeit them because of circumstances. We will only find them when we are completely surrendered to our God.

I have found just because we have given our lives to Christ does not automatically give us these three attributes. They come easy at the beginning, but after we have lived for God for a while we will find that hope, joy, and peace are things we will have to pursue. In Psalms it even says that we are to pursue peace.

These three attributes are anchors in turbulent times. They will be nourishment for the body, soul, and mind. Oftentimes our hope will be deferred. The fight for joy will sometimes leave us exhausted. It will feel like peace is far from us.

The armor gets heavy when we are fighting for our lives. Every piece is purposefully made with intentionality. Don't lay down that armor. Don't quit fighting for these three lifelines. Every battle is either won or lost in the mind! We must keep our minds free from the enemy's plots and schemes. Satan will never stop lying. His plan will never change: Steal, kill, and destroy.

Through this devotional I hope to offer encouraging scriptures and reflections to help reveal these staples in everyday life.

-Sheila

Part 1
Hopeful

Day 1

> **Hope deferred maketh the heart sick: but when the desire cometh, it is a tree of life.**
> Proverbs 13:12

This opening verse for devotional #9 shows how desperately we need hope in our lives. No matter how hard life gets, don't lose hope. This scripture explains the posture of our heart when hope is deferred. Sometimes our desires can be delayed. Our prayers may go unanswered for a season. Our spirit can get discouraged. The situation can weigh heavy in our minds. We know that the Bible is not referring to the literal heart muscle that pumps blood throughout our bodies. But like the heart muscle if something is off it will begin to show up in our life.

God's word never leaves us without a remedy. Our hope will be tested throughout life. It may seem all is lost. Time is passing. We are not getting younger. We need assurance that what we are hoping for will soon manifest or God will let us know it wasn't what we needed.

When the desire comes, it is a tree of life. A tree has many purposes. Fruit trees give us food. Certain trees are good for furniture, firewood, shade, and many other things. Hope keeps us growing strong.

Bee hopeful today.

Prayer (speak aloud)

Dear Lord, I have lost hope a few times in my life. I thank You for scriptures that give us strength to keep holding on. Hope is like an organ in our spiritual journey, we need it. My heart gets heavy. My soul gets discouraged. Hope seems far from me. What a comfort to know that when the desire comes, it will be life giving. All my hope is in You. Hope for breakthroughs. Hope for healing. Hope for our families. Hope for our wayward children to come back to You. Amen.

**Write about a time you felt all hope was lost.
How did that situation play out?**

Day 2

Now faith is the substance of things hoped for, the evidence of things not seen.

Hebrews 11:1

The eleventh chapter of Hebrews is like a weapon in our arsenal. It's known as the Hall of Faith chapter and is like a nail in a sure place. Stand on this verse. The chapter lists many characters throughout the Bible who pushed through adversity to carry the mantle of heaven in bringing people to God. Each person listed endured the pain of loss. The pain of waiting. The pain of being rejected. Moses was hidden for three months after he was born because he had been chosen by God to deliver the children of Israel. He would be eighty years old before he was ready to step into that role. Eighty years is a long time to stay in hope! What God called him to He brought to pass.

Take a few minutes and read all of Hebrews 11. Let it encourage you to hold on. These are models of faithfulness and hope.

What is faith? The substance of things hoped for. Hope and faith go hand in hand.

Prayer (speak aloud)

Thank You, God, for letting me know that no matter what my journey looks like I can hold on to hope. You kept Moses, Abraham, and many others while they waited for the promise to come to pass. I will keep hoping and believing that Your promises are true. I know that sometimes my journey is not very clear. I need You to guide me from day to day. I'm thankful that I have examples in the Bible of so many who held on to their hope. They held on till they saw Your hand moving in their lives. I will keep hoping. I will keep praying. Amen.

**Which person in Hebrews 11 stands out to you the most?
Why?
Write your own story of hope.**

_____
_____
_____
_____
_____
_____
_____
_____
_____
_____
_____
_____
_____
_____
_____
_____
_____
_____
_____
_____
_____
_____
_____
_____
_____
_____
_____

Day 3

For I know the thoughts that I think toward you, saith the Lord, thoughts of peace, and not of evil, to give you an expected end.

Jeremiah 29:11

In these Bee devotionals I always use the KJV, but the NIV version of this scripture is more familiar. It says "hope and a future." An "expected end" is merely another way of saying hope. We as children of God are always expecting a great ending. The children of Israel were being held captive in the Babylonian empire during this time of Jeremiah. To know that God had a plan for them was a relief, no doubt.

It's encouraging for us as we go through hard times. God told them to build houses, plant gardens, and eat the fruit of them. He told them to take wives and have children so that they may increase while they were there even in captivity. In praying peace for the city they would also have peace.

There is so much hope in this scripture. We must continue to press on no matter the circumstance. We will not see the birth of our dreams without the accompanying birthing pains. God is not mad at us. He is mad about us. Because we live in this broken world we see and feel the effects of it. God has a plan for us to live with hope and peace.

Prayer (speak aloud)

Lord, the hope You have given me in this story is so encouraging. I will do what You tell me to do even when things are uncertain. Help me to keep building, to keep planting, and most of all keep believing. You have promised a future that is full of hope. Hope for my children. Hope for my journey. I will keep expecting the best. What a blessed assurance that even in the midst of captivity You are working behind the scenes. You have my back. In the end I win. Amen.

**Will you keep building, planting, and believing while you go through hard times?
Write what you hope to see manifest in your life.**

Day 4

But they that wait upon the L%%ORD%% shall renew their strength; they shall mount up with wings as eagles; they shall run, and not be weary; and they shall walk, and not faint.

Isaiah 40:31

Waiting on the Lord renews our strength. When we're waiting, we're hoping. Even though the word *hope* is not mentioned in this scripture, it definitely shouts hope.

As we hope in the Lord for the turn around, the breakthrough, the healing, we need our strength renewed. When we're waiting, we're resting, and rest allows us to keep the pace. Without rest, we get worn down and are not at our best.

Eagles are among my favorite birds. It's no secret why God refers to the eagle throughout scripture for our learning. They are massive in size. They don't just fly, they soar. They are often alone. They can spot their prey up to four miles away. That's an unbelievable vision. The eagle uses the storm to its advantage. We can have unshakable faith and hope when we see ourselves having these qualities.

Whether you run, walk, or crawl, don't quit hoping while you wait.

Prayer (speak aloud)

Thank You Father, for the blessed hope I find in Your Word. Thank You for strength when I'm weak. Through the Spirit I can mount up with wings as eagles. I can soar above the pressures that life brings. I can run and not be weary. I can walk and not faint. Help me to wait with expectancy. Help me to keep my hope intact. You have promised to keep us through trials. Your presence is always there when we face uncertainty. When I go through the fire You are there. When I go through deep waters You are there. Sometimes when the waves are beating upon my boat my hope can get weak. When I am weak You are strong. Amen.

**Have you ever read up on eagles?
It's a great comparison for our journey on this earth.
Journal your own thoughts on this scripture.**

Day 5

And when neither sun nor stars in many days appeared, and no small tempest lay on us, all hope that we should be saved was then taken away.

Acts 27:20

Paul was a prisoner on a ship that was headed for destruction. They had already sailed a few places safely. The centurion that was placed over Paul showed favor to him at one of the stops, even allowing him to go unto his friends and refresh himself. They were getting ready to sail out from a different place. Paul warned them that it's not safe to sail. The centurion ignored the warning and set sail anyway.

The ship began to be tossed to and fro in the storm. (Have you ever felt like you were on a ship being tossed around? We probably all have!) This was a pretty hopeless situation. No stars, no sun for days. All hope was taken away. Paul got a word from God that no lives would be lost. He tells them to be of good cheer. The ship was torn apart in the storm, just like Paul said. No lives were lost because Paul received hope in a hopeless time. An angel of God stood before him in the middle of all this chaos and gave specific instructions to keep them all alive.

Acts 27 is a great story of hope in what seemed a hopeless and desperate case.

Prayer (speak aloud)

Thank You Lord for the example of Paul. This was just one of the many times that You brought hope into Paul's journey. Help me to look to You when the storms of life are beating on my ship. Help me believe that You are on the ship with me. Thank You for always being with me. Sometimes it feels like You are thousands of miles away. The Word tells me that is not true. I'm thankful for hope. Hope in the prayers I've prayed. Hope in the seeds I've sown. Hope in the middle of dark times. Hope in the testimonies in my own life as well as others. All my hope is in You. Amen.

**Read the whole chapter of Acts 27 if you can.
Can you relate to Paul?
Journal about a time that you lost hope and God came through.**

_____
_____
_____
_____
_____
_____
_____
_____
_____
_____
_____
_____
_____
_____
_____
_____
_____
_____
_____
_____
_____
_____
_____
_____

Day 6

For there is hope of a tree, if it be cut down, that it will sprout again, and that the tender branch thereof will not cease.
8. Though the root thereof wax old in the earth, and the stock thereof
die in the ground;
9. Yet through the scent of water it will bud, and bring forth boughs like a plant.

Job 14:7–9

We all know that if you want to get rid of weeds they must be pulled up by the roots. The old saying, "as long as there is breath there is hope," falls in line with this passage. Though the tree was cut down, there is still hope lying dormant in the roots. That tree may also find hope in the seeds it shed into the earth.

We all have seen tree stumps with little branches sprouting from them. The stump looks dead. No life seems to be left in it. Hidden underground is a root. A piece of life that is unseen by the natural eye. A root called hope. If that root just gets the scent of water it will sprout again.

Things can seem hopeless. A sickness. A death. A number of circumstances can arise in our lives. Through a word, through a phone call, a dream, God can water that root of hope. Your heart could learn to beat again. Branches can sprout from that stump.

Believe that God is watering your hope.

Prayer (speak aloud)

God, You have put hope back in my hopelessness many times. My hope has been like that tree stump. Seemingly no hope. What assurance You have given me in these scriptures. I have felt that hopeless despair. I have faced some uncertain times. God, You keep watering that root of hope. You keep showing me Your love. You keep encouraging me through others. I read story after story in Your Word that keeps me expecting those branches to sprout again. Even when Job lost all hope, You showed up and showed out on his behalf. I will always look for that little ray of hope to keep my faith intact. Amen.

**Have you ever pulled weeds? Have they come back?
Have you ever seen a tree stump with branches sprouting?
What are some ways that God has helped you regain hope?**

Day 7

And not only so, but we glory in tribulations also: knowing that tribulation worketh patience;
4. And patience, experience; and experience, hope:
5. And hope maketh not ashamed; because the love of God is shed abroad in our hearts by the Holy Ghost which is given unto us.

Romans 5:3–5

It seems that hope is something that we learn to lean into as we travel this road called life. To need hope we must experience hopeless situations. Tribulation is not the word we really want to hear. We know that God tells us we shall have tribulation. Be of good cheer though, because God has overcome the world.

Through each challenge that life brings us to, our hope will be strengthened. Patience is a fruit of the spirit. That means we will face times of waiting. Nothing like waiting to build up that patience muscle. Of course as we wait we will experience different emotions. We will question the reason for certain trials. We will wonder where God is.

Verse 5 should build our faith and confidence. Hope maketh not ashamed. Why? Because God loves us. He cares. He's working something far greater in our spirits than our natural man can comprehend. He is more concerned about your character than your comfort. It doesn't feel good when we are learning what hope really means. Remember, God is growing you through this thing we call hope.

Prayer (speak aloud)

Tribulation, patience, and experience are not the most encouraging words. Through these words You teach me to have hope. Thank You for the wisdom to see that even in the hard season there is hope. God, Your ways are much higher than mine. Your thoughts are above my thoughts. You see the end from the beginning. You have my best interest in mind. Sometimes hope can seem far away. You said You will never leave me, which means hope is always there. You are hope. Thank You God that when I am in a season of waiting or simply being still I can stay hopeful because of Your Word. Amen.

**Write about some experiences that taught you to stay hopeful.
Have you ever felt ashamed for waiting on God?**

Day 8

Rejoice not against me, O mine enemy: when I fall, I shall arise; when I sit in darkness, the Lord shall be a light unto me.

Micah 7:8

When I fall, not if I fall.

We will fall. The human side of us will fall and come up short more times than we would like to admit. The hope that is buried in this verse should encourage every believer. The devil laughs every time we stumble and fall. He is like a roaring lion waiting to pounce on us after we have given in to some temptation. Satan is the only one that will keep pushing you to avenge yourself or tempt you to do that wrong, then condemn you.

When we stumble even in the natural, it can be because we are moving around in the dark. God says even in the darkness He is the light. When we fall there is hope. His Word is our light. His forgiveness is our hope. The enemy can not keep us down as long as we keep that lifeline open to our Heavenly Father.

Rejoice not against me Satan. God has my back.

Prayer (speak aloud)

Thank You dear God for Micah 7:8. You knew I would fall. Not only fall but make horrible mistakes. Thank You for the light that shines so bright even in the darkest times. Thank You for the hope that is being heard in this verse. The enemy is always one step behind me hoping I will fall. He tries to surround me with hopeless situations daily. Sometimes I fall for his schemes. I get discouraged when my prayers are not being answered. I lose hope when the wait is longer than I expected. The joy that belongs to me seems to be a million miles away. My hope gets deferred. The darkness is thick. Don't rejoice too soon Satan. God is my help in times of trouble. A light of hope. Amen.

**Journal about a time you stumbled in the dark in your walk with God.
What was the hope that helped you to arise?**

Day 9

And said, Naked came I out of my mother's womb, and naked shall I return thither: the LORD gave, and the LORD hath taken away; blessed be the name of the LORD.

Job 1:21

There are many people in the Bible who have stories of hope. We can easily see that Job was in a seemingly hopeless season. I chose Job because his journey is a gut wrenching heartbreak one after another. The only thing that was not taken was his wife. She saw his pain and misery. Remember, those were her children too. To curse God and die was probably not what Job expected to hear. She offered no hope.

Let's not forget Job's friends. With friends like that who needs enemies, right? They were accusing him of failing somewhere. No hope came from them either. Job didn't even offer much hope for his own story. He was questioning everything. Why was he born? Why didn't he die in his mother's womb? That sounds pretty hopeless.

The verse we shared today put what hope Job had in one statement, "The Lord gave, and the Lord hath taken away; blessed be the name of the Lord".

In the end Job found hope in God's faithfulness. Job didn't throw in the towel. He got double for his trouble.

Prayer (speak aloud)

Dear Lord, I hope I never have to face what Job faced. If I do I pray that I can hang on to the end. Thank You for your unwavering love to me. Thank You for showing me through stories like this that I can make it no matter how hopeless my situation is. I know Satan is always accusing You of keeping me down. He tries to wear me down with thoughts of discouragement. He says You don't care about me or I wouldn't be facing this heartache. The enemy does his job well. When the enemy makes me feel hopeless, I will call out to You. Thank You God that if I hold on my reward will be out of this world. Amen.

**How do you feel about the story of Job?
Can you relate to him?**

Day 10

(As it is written, I have made thee a father of many nations,) before him whom he believed, even God, who quickeneth the dead, and calleth those things which be not as though they were. 18. Who against hope believed in hope, that he might become the father of many nations; according to that which was spoken, So shall thy seed be.

Romans 4:17–18

We can't talk about hope without the story of Abraham. Look at verse 18. Abraham held onto hope. In the natural Abraham and Sarah were past child bearing years. We can see why Abraham stated the obvious. At 75 years old a promise was given to him. Yet, another 25 years would come and go before this miracle would take place. When the verse says quickeneth the dead, that was referring to Abraham being past the age to bear children.

We see faith and hope coming together in this story. Faith by speaking those things that "be not as though they were." Our hope should be lifted up by just reading and hearing the heart of Abraham.

We may not be hoping for children. We may be hoping for a breakthrough in some other area. If you got a word from God, a dream or desire you want to see come to pass then let this passage fill you with hope. His timing is perfect. His ways are perfect. We will testify of his goodness. Stay hopeful.

Prayer (speak aloud)

God I thank You for giving me examples like Abraham to build my hope. I will call those things that are not as though they are. I have faith that You will finish in me what You started. I am asking You to move for me. Give me the strength to keep holding on. Even now I feel my hope is weak. When I am weak You are strong. I know people of the world think I am foolish for believing in my dreams. I will be a light in someone's darkness. I will speak words in due season to those who have lost hope. My life will be a living testimony of the faithfulness of You. Encourage me today to keep hoping and never give up. Amen.

What are you believing for that seems hopeless? Remind God of His faithfulness to others and ask Him not to forget you.

Part 2
Joyful

Day 11

Then he said unto them, Go your way, eat the fat, and drink the sweet, and send portions unto them for whom nothing is prepared: for this day is holy unto our Lord: neither be ye sorry; for the joy of the Lord is your strength.

Nehemiah 8:10

We have moved into part two with being joyful. When we keep joy in our hearts then hope will be easier.

Ezra the priest is reading the book of the law of Moses. If you ever wonder why preachers stand behind pulpits and the congregation stands I encourage you to read this chapter. Ezra read the law and gave the sense of it. He helped them to understand what they were hearing. It seems that they had not been following the law. We can see how this plays out for them by comparing it to our own lives.

It's not always joyous when God reveals our wrongs. Ezra tells them to not be sad. God's Word is our instruction manual, and if we follow the directions we will get to our appointed destination. It is for our own good.

Ezra says be joyful. That joy will be your strength. Even though the law was calling them out it was for their good. He tells them to eat and be merry. Share your blessing with others. When we obey God's Word it becomes our joy.

Prayer (speak aloud)

The way of the Lord is the way of wisdom. Thank You God for the wisdom to know that Your law is for my good. I will stay joyful knowing that Your plan for me is good. I don't always like the chastening that I receive. When Your Word reveals my slackness it can be challenging to correct it. I know that if I will diligently follow after what is right then joy will be my portion. I will always stand on this truth that the joy of the Lord is my strength. Help me to show others that no matter how hard life gets that joy can be found in serving You. Even in my learning and growing season I will share the blessing of God with others. Because I know by helping others my joy will be strengthened. Amen.

**Name something that God revealed to you that yielded joy after the fact.
What are some areas in your life that bring you joy?**

Day 12

Thou wilt shew me the path of life: in thy presence is fulness of joy; at thy right hand there are pleasures for evermore.

Psalm 16:11

Joy can be found in many areas of our life. When we are on vacation, joy is sure to be in the midst. A new baby is born, the mother is joyful. Many are joyful around the holidays. Pretty lights twinkling. The sound of Christmas music in the stores. Life is full of joyous moments. One of the greatest joys that can't be compared to is being in the presence of the Lord.

In God's presence you will find a peace that is unmatched. We will find our path easier when we dwell in His presence. "Right hand" often refers to the power of God. At His right hand we can find happiness that no person can take away.

In this same chapter verse 9 says, "therefore my heart is glad, and my glory rejoiceth: my flesh also shall rest in hope." I love how it refers to our flesh as well. Yes, our spirits can be joyful. We live in everyday life right now and sometimes even our flesh needs assurance. Maybe you are in a season that seems less than joyful.

Don't feel discouraged, keep the faith, keep believing, keep pushing, whatever you do don't lose your joy.

Prayer (speak aloud)

God Your presence is what I long for. When I dwell in Your presence I find the joy that You want me to have. Thank You God that even when I'm slacking on my end that You always let me know that I can still have joy in my soul. My heart rejoices in Thy presence. My life is meaningless without You. Moses said if Your presence doesn't go with me I don't even want to go. I feel the same as Moses. Your Word lets me know that You are with me at all times. No matter how hard life gets. No matter how hopeless the situation seems. I never want to lose my joy. At Your right hand are pleasures forever more. Amen.

**Is joy a constant in your life?
I believe that we can always find joy even in the midst of hard times.
Journal about some times that you had to find joy in the process.**

Day 13

**My brethren, count it all joy when ye fall into divers temptations;
3. Knowing this, that the trying of your faith worketh patience.
4. But let patience have her perfect work, that ye may be perfect and entire, wanting nothing.**

James 1:2–4

I will admit this passage of scripture has always challenged me. Count it all joy when trouble comes!

Our lives are full of temptation. Many times we think of temptation as lust for another person, lust for the gain of this world. Yes, those temptations are there. We also are tempted to lose hope. We are tempted to lose faith when the battle grows long and weary. We can see that God did not leave us without hope.

When we are tried our faith can be strengthened. We learn to be more patient. We will see the hand of God working on us and through us. The quote about He's more concerned about your character than your comfort can be found in James. We as humans always want the easy way out. We would like God to just let us have all the things we need to be a Christian. For the most part there is work for us to do. We are to be joyful even in the hard seasons. One reason is it not only helps us to grow in our own journey, it helps others to find the joy they need to press on.

Let us count it all Joy!

Prayer (speak aloud)

Lord, help me to find joy in the hard times. Help me to realize that it's not just about me when I face temptations. As I learn patience. As I stand in the midst of heartache and trauma let me find the joy that will shine through the darkness. I pray that the joy that goes before me will be the light that someone else needs. I'm thankful for these scriptures because it's not always easy to find the silver lining when the storm is beating me up. Help me to keep my eyes on You when life is being difficult. Life is hard by default. Thank You God that there is a button called joy that I can change the setting. My hope, my joy, and my peace are all in You. Amen.

**Do you have a tendency to look for joy no matter what is going on?
Always remember that when the situation is happening, God is doing a work in you.
Journal your own reflections and insights.**

Day 14

Every man also to whom God hath given riches and wealth, and hath given him power to eat thereof, and to take his portion, and to rejoice in his labour; this is the gift of God. 20. For he shall not much remember the days of his life; because God answereth him in the joy of his heart.

Ecclesiastes 5:19–20

To have joy is a gift from God. Ecclesiastes is full of uncertainty. It seems to leave us wondering about our life here on earth. Solomon wasted the gifts that God bestowed upon him. We see his journey left him a little disheartened. Even though Solomon has seen his days of trouble he also has seen the goodness of God.

Only by God do we enjoy the labor of our hands. If God has given us riches and wealth, this is a gift. He will let us take our portion. In the world we live in now it's hard to find joy. Yet God has given us a hope that even though we will face dark times we won't remember them. Why? Because God will move on our behalf.

He will answer us with His Word. He will bring joy into our hearts. He will go before us. He will send His angels to keep us in all our ways. He will let His Spirit rest on us and in us. That my friend is joy. We can have the joy of the Lord in all circumstances. Remember trouble doesn't last always. And joy will come in the morning.

May your tomorrows be better than your yesterdays.

Prayer (speak aloud)

How wonderful You are God to let me have joy. Joy in my family. Joy in my labor. Joy in my everyday life. You gave me this gift called time. You give me hope. I know that life can be hard sometimes. It can keep me stuck. I just want to praise You for the courage to keep moving forward. Thank You for the light at the end of the tunnel. Sometimes that light is joy, hope, and peace. Sometimes it's a text from a friend. Sometimes it's a smile from a stranger. Sometimes it's tears rolling down my cheek while I'm traveling to another town. Sometimes it's Your presence filling my bathroom while I listen to worship music. I thank You for this unspeakable joy. Amen.

**What do you think of Solomon in this book?
Can you see yourself in Solomon's journey?
Some days are better than others!**

Day 15

These things have I spoken unto you, that my joy might remain in you, and that your joy might be full.

John 15:11

What things is John talking about? The whole chapter is laced with hope and joy. I love this chapter because it gives us a clear understanding of how to keep joy in our lives. Jesus is the vine and we are the branches. He is the source of our joy. If we don't stay connected to Him we will lose our joy. Our branch will wither and die. That is what happens in our own life, we start to die. Not a physical death but a spiritual death. The only true joy we have is staying connected to Him.

We must realize that God knows what is best for us. He cuts away the extra foliage to produce more fruit. I read that sometimes the vinedresser will even cut off smaller clusters of grapes so that the bigger ones are not competing with them. This will produce bigger and sweeter grapes.

Maybe we have too much weighing us down. So busy for God that we have no time for Him. God wants His joy to remain in us. When His joy remains in us we are full of hope and faith. I'm going to stay connected to the vine so I can stay joyful.

Prayer (speak aloud)

Dear God, help me to see when I'm getting too busy. You are the vinedresser of my soul. You are my source of joy. As long as I allow You to be the head of my life, my joy will be full. I have a lot of things competing against my walk with You. I want Your joy to remain in me. You were able to endure the cross, scorning, and shame for the joy that was set before You. You died for my sins. You took stripes on Your back. Nails were driven through Your hands and feet. You were mocked and spit on. You did all that so my joy might be full. The joy of the Lord is my strength. Amen.

Have you ever felt God pruning your branch? When he gets through it will yield bigger and better fruit. Stay connected to the vine!

Day 16

Although the fig tree shall not blossom, neither shall fruit be in the vines; the labour of the olive shall fail, and the fields shall yield no meat; the flock shall be cut off from the fold, and there shall be no herd in the stalls: 18. Yet I will rejoice in the Lord, I will joy in the God of my salvation.

Habakkuk 3:17–18

My former late pastor used to say, "it's hard to stay joyful when the bulldog has you by the seat of your britches." The language in the KJV has always been a little extra for me. It seems to go straight for the throat. Habakkuk is praying in this chapter. You can hear his pain, he does not understand the dilemma they are in. Why won't God come and rescue them now and not later?

We can all relate to this desperate prayer. Things are not good. Even now in this era we see so much heartache. We feel the darkness around us, the Bible said we would. I'm thankful for these scriptures. They speak of hard times, even lack. When nothing is yielding like it should. No fruit on the vines. No calves are being birthed. The stalls are empty. That is a pretty drastic time. Yet, I will rejoice in the Lord. I will hold on to my joy. Why? Because God cannot lie. He will vindicate His children who cry day and night.

Let's keep our hopes up. Let's rejoice for our future is already established on the promises of God. Let's stay joyful even when life isn't being kind to us.

Prayer (speak aloud)

I have gone days that it didn't seem like You were there. I have been in those seasons of drought. Thank You God for giving me hope through Habakkuk's prayer. I've lost friends along the way. I've lost some things on this road of life. I've been to the graveyard laying my loved ones to rest. I've prayed oh God where are You. I want to be strong like Habakkuk. Praise You in the hard season. Rejoice even when I'm not seeing Your hand in my life at the moment. Because I know joy will come in the morning. You won't leave me like this. Your Word is a light unto my path. I will keep my eyes on the prize. Nothing or no one will steal my joy. Amen.

**Have you ever been in the trenches of life and asked "God, where are You?"
My dear reader, I have been there more times than I want to admit.
Journal and pray today. Release it to God.**

Day 17

3. The Lord hath done great things for us; whereof we are glad.
5. They that sow in tears shall reap in joy.
6. He that goeth forth and weepeth, bearing precious seed, shall doubtless come again with rejoicing, bringing his sheaves with him.

Psalm 126:3, 5–6

What a trade. Sowing tears, reaping in joy. One thing about God's Word is it never leaves us without hope. Just like faith without works is dead, so is our joy.

There is an old gospel song that I didn't quite understand when I was younger. Maybe you have heard of it. Thank You For The Valley written by Dottie Rambo. Do yourself a favor and look it up on YouTube. Thanking God for a valley. Thanking Him for everytime the sun didn't shine. Eph. 5:20 tells us to give thanks always for all things. First Thessalonians 5:18 says in everything give thanks for this is the will of God concerning us.

Sometimes we will sow in tears. Sometimes we will weep. The hard days will make us appreciate the good days. When we take the time to look at the grand picture we can see the hand of God on and in our life. Keep planting those tears. Remember they are bottled up in Heaven. He doesn't forget them. Verse 3 says the Lord has done great things for us; whereof we are glad.

We wouldn't know what joy felt like if we never had a problem. Even though we struggle in this life, there is joy for God's people. Be encouraged by this passage today. Let's choose joy.

Prayer (speak aloud)

God I have sowed many tears throughout my lifetime. I thank You for allowing those tears to be the water for the harvest of joy. You have been so good to me. You have done great things whereof I am glad. Like the song says, I thank You for the valley I walk through today. In the valley are streams of living water. In the valley the grass is lush and green. When the clouds hang low. The storms rage. The sun won't shine for days. I know that behind all those clouds, the sun is shining. I know that joy is my portion. Thank You for trading my tears of sorrow for tears of joy. Amen.

**What comes to mind after reading this passage?
Have you ever gone through a hard season to find out later it was for your good.
Write about a time you sowed in tears and God brought joy from it.**

Day 18

14. Sing, O daughter of Zion; shout, O Israel; be glad and rejoice with all the heart, O daughter of Jerusalem.

17. The Lord thy God in the midst of thee is mighty; he will save, he will rejoice over thee with joy; he will rest in his love, he will joy over thee with singing.

Zephaniah 3:14, 17

Can you imagine the Lord singing over us with joy? He tells us to sing, shout, and rejoice with all our heart.

One thing that I have learned on this Christian walk is when a subject is repeated in the Bible over and over it's a sure sign of significance. Praising God, singing and lifting our voices, is a pattern for victory. It will not only lift us up, it will help others.

Paul and Silas sang and praised God at the midnight hour. They were chained up in the prison. All the doors opened when they sang and praised God. Not just their doors, all the doors.

It's like a recipe for winning. God sees us giving Him praise even when we are in the battle. It causes Him to respond with the same joy. This passage says He will be in the midst of us. God truly loves us. He desires our praise. So much so that the Word says He inhabits our praise.

True growth in God will produce singing and praising in our midnight hour. True growth will produce joy even when things are not so joyful. Let's rest in His love for us. Open the ears of your heart and hear Him singing over you with joy.

Prayer (speak aloud)

I lift You up today, God. I sing and rejoice for Your grace and mercy. Thank You for being in the midst of my journey. I want to sing and praise You even when it feels like I'm in a prison. I know that You inhabit my praises. I know that you rejoice over me with joy. I want my praise to set other people free, just like Paul and Silas. My family is counting on me to keep my joy. My friends need me to keep my joy. I'm thankful for the Word that encourages me to rest in Your love. I don't know what song You are singing over me. I just enjoy knowing that You have joy in my walk with You. Amen.

**What song comes to your mind that God might be singing over you?
Have you ever thought about how your joy can open other people's doors?
Write about the joy you have today.**

Day 19

For ye shall go out with joy, and be led forth with peace: the mountains and the hills shall break forth before you into singing, and all the trees of the field shall clap their hands.

Isaiah 55:12

To appreciate verse 12 we should consider verses 8–11. Our thoughts are not His thoughts. Our ways are not His ways. Sometimes when life is seemingly beating us up, when our prayers go unanswered, in those times we often find God working behind the scenes. He can take the problem and work it for our good.

Verses 10 & 11 speak about nature bringing snow and rain. We don't always like the rain or the snow. God lets us know that they come to benefit us. They water the valley's. They don't return void.

These passages of scriptures help us to find joy even in uncertain times. We see God using His creation to teach us about joy. Mountains, hills, and trees are often symbolic to His people. We can break forth into singing. Nature has its own rhythm of praising God. The trees clap their hands (leaves move in the wind). Birds praise God through their chirping.

Everything in nature has a purpose. Though the trees, mountains, and hills don't have souls, they still have life. They are examples of true joy and peace.

Prayer (speak aloud)

Thank You God for the joy that flows through my life. I don't want the trees to out do me. I don't want a rock to cry out in my place. I want to sing and praise You with all my heart. I was born to worship You. I was born to serve You. I want to let the life You have blessed me with to be a testimony for others. Help me to fulfill the purpose that You have brought me into this earth for. I thank You for the beauty of nature. I see You in the warm sunshine. I see You in the soft rain. I see you when winter ends and spring begins to break forth. It's nature being joyful. I choose to have joy. Amen.

What do you see in nature that reminds you of God's plan? Have you ever thought about the trees clapping their hands? Write your own nature's story so you can see joy in it.

Day 20

For his anger endureth but a moment; in his favour is life: weeping may endure for a night, but joy cometh in the morning.

Psalm 30:5

Weeping may endure for a night. Let's be real here, sometimes it's many nights. What do we do when the morning comes and nothing has changed? What do we do when weeks go by and we are still weeping? We keep believing that the Word is true.

The morning in this passage doesn't necessarily refer to the natural sunrise. It is a state of being. In the natural we love to see the daylight after a hard night. Especially after a night of rain, storms, and wind. We see that God's anger doesn't last. Favor and joy flows from His goodness.

David reflects on the goodness of God at the beginning of this chapter. He thanks God for letting him live. He is praising God for not letting his foes rejoice over him. David said, "God thou has healed me." David was a man who felt joy, pain and sorrow. Yet he knew that God was merciful.

We must know that joy is a decision. Every day may not be good. Every situation doesn't always end well. Sometimes we will simply stand on past victories. Keep crying out to God. Don't quit.

Joy will come in the morning!

Prayer (speak aloud)

God, I have wept bitter tears. My heart has been broken. I have seen hard times in my life. I also have seen You move miraculously. You have been there time and time again. Working all things for my good. You made a way when it felt impossible. You lifted my spirit when I was discouraged. This joy that comes from You doesn't hinge on the outcomes of my expectations. When I go through the fire. When I go through deep waters. When I walk through the valley. It's Your joy that keeps me. Knowing that You are always with me helps me to keep putting one foot in front of the other. I'm thankful for the joy of the lord. Amen.

**What is something you do to help you get through a hard season?
Write about past victories. Review them often.**

Part 3
Peaceful

Day 21

**13. Keep thy tongue from evil, and thy lips from speaking guile.
14. Depart from evil, and do good; seek peace, and pursue it.**

Psalm 34:13–14

Verse 12 is asking a question: What man is he that desireth life, and loveth many days, that he may see good? Who doesn't want peace to be at the center of their life? Verses 13 & 14 give us the antidote to having peace in our lives.

The tongue is an unruly evil (James 3:8). The Bible tells us no man can tame it. It takes the spirit of God helping us. Even then we have to allow God to nudge us. When we let God be the head of our life we will be able to discern what spirit is trying to control us. We have to depart from evil. Do good. Seek peace and pursue it. Pursue is an action word. We have to go after it.

Peace will not automatically come naturally for us. As humans we want things to go our way. Even when someone has done you wrong God wants us to seek peace. This is not always easy. A few years back my husband sold a side by side (it was an older one). He did not ask me about it, and I was so hurt. I loved that side by side. I rode the grandkids in it. I used it to pick up sticks before I mowed. It wasn't easy to have peace in my spirit. That same week as I was venting to God He dropped these scriptures in my heart. I had to let it go and seek peace. Not just seek it, pursue it.

Prayer (speak aloud)

Thank You, Father, for helping me when I am at a loss for words. Thank You for a peace that the world can't understand. I don't always get it right. Some days I struggle with doing good. I struggle with seeking peace. I definitely need help pursuing it. Peace is often like joy, it's a choice. I know without Your help I can't win that battle. I need You to remind me often how to choose peace. Thank You that when I am weak You are strong. When I am hurt or discouraged, surround me with that perfect peace. Help me remember that You are peace. I can look into Your Word and find the answer. Amen.

**Write about a time that you had to seek peace.
Have you ever had to pursue it?**

Day 22

Thou wilt keep him in perfect peace, whose mind is stayed on thee: because he trusteth in thee.

Isaiah 26:3

There is peace then there is perfect peace. Perfect often signifies a state of completeness, wholeness, and maturity. It seems the Bible is clear that we have a part to play in this area of peace. On day 21 we see *seek* and *pursue* are verbs.

When we fill our heart with the Word we can fight from a more peaceful place. The Word lets us know how to obtain this perfect peace. Our minds must stay on the Lord. We will draw closer to God. Our trust will be like a safety net.

One reason the Word brings peace is because it's like medicine. It heals our troubled minds. It soothes our doubts. It will calm our fears because it is rooted in truth. Truth that will trump even facts with supernatural power.

It's a fact that our world is broken. We are plagued with heartaches. We see chaos and confusion every day. Yet, we as the children of God can have perfect peace in the midst of it all. We have to keep our mind stayed on Him.

Prayer (speak aloud)

God of peace, that is who You are. Peace in the midst of trouble. Peace in the middle of the storm. Peace when sickness is plaguing my body. Thank You God for showing me how to have peace at all times. Your Word comforts me when I'm grieving. In the book of Psalms it says I can rejoice at thy Word as one that has found great spoil. What a comfort knowing that after the battle, after the victory I can walk away with everything I need to sustain my journey. Thank You, God, for peace beyond my own understanding. Thank You for keeping me in these troublesome times. There is nothing to compare the peace that I find in You. Amen.

**Do you have perfect peace?
What seems to be the biggest peace-stealer in
your walk with God?
Let's keep our minds on Him (Word).**

Day 23

1. My son, forget not my law; but let thine heart keep my commandments: 2. For length of days, and long life, and peace, shall they add to thee.

Proverbs 3:1–2

What a promise! Again we see the Word is our arsenal.

These same instructions are found throughout the Word. Forget not His law. Keep it in thy heart. How do we get it in our hearts? We must read it. Not only read it, pray for understanding. We can read the Bible daily and still live defeated if we don't let it get in our hearts. This is important because the more we know the easier we can withstand the attacks of the enemy. The more we know the more peace we will have.

Peace in your life helps your physical body as well. Research has shown us that stress, worry, and grief can affect us in every area of our life. When we keep His Word in our hearts we are setting ourselves up for a longer life span. The more you know and understand the less the Devil can get the upper hand over you.

My dear readers, peace is our medicine. It can keep blood pressure down. It can keep your heart from getting out of whack. The peace of God is a multi-faceted gem. It's a priceless treasure.

Prayer (speak aloud)

God, I thank You for peace. When I get too busy doing other things, nudge me. I want the long life and peace that Your Word says I can have. I will keep Your commandments. I won't forget Your law. I know that Your law is for my own good. If I do good to others, good will come back to me. The law of sowing and reaping is a solid truth that I can hold on to. Each truth that I find in Your Word is a step on the ladder to this undeniable peace. Oh what peace I forfeit when I stay in darkness. What peace I forfeit when I don't seek to know Your Word. You have given me Your Word as a shield and sword. With this understanding I can have peace at all times. Amen.

Did you know that God gives us different ways to add days to our life?
Did you know that we can obtain peace through His Word?
Write a passage of scriptures that brings you peace.

Day 24

Peace I leave with you, my peace I give unto you: not as the world giveth, give I unto you. Let not your heart be troubled, neither let it be afraid.

John 14:27

There is a peace that comes from God that is unexplainable. It's a priceless treasure.

There is no generic peace. We can do a lot of things. Go to a lot of places. Enjoy some of the most incredible adventures. Vacations, beaches, and seeing views from the highest mountains. All of this can make us happy. This form of happiness and peace is from the world. That doesn't mean it's a bad thing. We just can't make that our only source. Many wealthy famous people are in the grave today because they didn't have the peace that comes from above.

The pure peace of God will keep you when your whole world is turned upside down. God's peace will calm a troubled heart. It will drive fear from your life. We all have had our world to be shattered in one way or another. Loss of loved ones. Divorces. Betrayal. Fires, tornados, and floods. Our world is full of chaos. The Bible is being fulfilled right before our eyes.

Thank God for this peace. Jesus Christ is our peace. He comforts, He guides, He will go to the ends of the earth with us. That my friend, is genuine peace.

Prayer (speak aloud)

I praise You today God for this peace. You have taught me how to receive this peace. The enemy of my soul continues to throw curve balls in my path. He paints a picture of doom and gloom all around me. I am thankful for the natural beauty that You have created. I love watching a creek flow through a valley. The water flowing over the rocks. The sound of rain on a metal roof. Wind chimes making a beautiful sound. How good You are to me. I have seen your goodness in my life. I have felt Your presence in my most troubled times. I believe this is the peace You give us. A peace that is truly priceless. Amen.

Can you think of some times that the peace of God kept you? Take a little time and reminisce about those times. What was going on? Where did God show up?

Day 25

17. For the kingdom of God is not meat and drink; but righteousness, and peace, and joy in the Holy Ghost.
19. Let us therefore follow after the things which make for peace, and things wherewith one may edify another.

Romans 14:17,19

We all need peace. We need it in our families, on our jobs, on the roads. We can see even in this passage we can't hang our peace on things or events.

God's kingdom has a different path to peace. The righteousness of God will bring peace simply doing the right things. The spirit of God brings peace and joy. There are many opportunities to let life overwhelm us. We have to follow after the things that make for peace. We have to seek to find a common ground while going about our daily tasks.

Many people are living on the edge of losing their grip at any given moment. Verse 19 says let us look for ways to be at peace with others. Peace is often on the back burner in many lives. The peace of God that radiates from our own lives will shine through the darkness that is invading our workplaces, our schools, even our homes.

Peace will have to be chosen. It will have to be pursued. The enemy has come to steal, kill and destroy. If he can steal our peace he has got his foot in the door.

Let peace reign in your life today. Choose peace.

Prayer (speak aloud)

Heavenly Father I praise You for the peace that I find daily. Help me to follow after the things that bring peace. Help me to be an example of this great peace. Let my life speak peace. I know that when I let peace have its way in my life, I will edify others. When my workplace is chaotic, let me be the peace. When my family is going through hard times, let me be the peace. No matter what the enemy throws at me I will look to You for my peace. I know the only real peace I have is You. Amen.

Have you ever had to speak peace into a chaotic situation? What is something you do that helps to bring calmness? When you choose peace it affects others.

Day 26

14. And above all these things put on charity, which is the bond of perfectness.
15. And let the peace of God rule in your hearts, to the which also ye are called in one body; and be ye thankful.
16. Let the word of Christ dwell in you richly in all wisdom; teaching and admonishing one another in psalms and hymns and spiritual songs, singing with grace in your hearts to the Lord.

Colossians 3:14–16

We can see that our peace affects others as well as ourselves. With the peace of God in our hearts we can be more thankful.

The world we are living in today needs us to show forth the love of God. Have you ever been in the presence of someone that radiates peace? They are usually singing, humming, and being joyful. For just a little while you can forget about the troubles that are knocking at your door. We are called to live in this peace that the world can't comprehend. Does this mean we don't face heartaches? Yes we all do.

Tragedy comes to every family. Let me add that just because we live for God does not exempt us from problems. Sometimes the child of God will fight harder than those that are not sold out to God. Why? Because peace is a priceless commodity that isn't just lying around in abundance. Remember we have to pursue it.

There is no doubt why the enemy targets this area of our life. Many things in our lives are centered around this beautiful peace.

Prayer (speak aloud)

I will let Your peace rule in my heart. I will be thankful. Thank You for peace, wisdom, and understanding. My life is nothing without You. I will purposely sing and praise You throughout my day. I will lift up Your name in the presence of the enemy. Thank You God for giving me this weapon called peace. It's a priceless treasure. Satan hates us because we are your workmanship. He sets out to steal, kill, and destroy. Send Your angels to help me fight against this unseen force trying to steal my hope, joy, and peace. Satan is relentless. He hits below the belt. Attacks my marriage, my children, my health, and my finances. On the cross You cried out it is finished. That is my truth. You won the battle for me. Amen.

**Why do you think Satan works overtime trying to steal your peace?
What is a touchy area that always seems to pull on you?
Decree today that he is a liar and you already won!**

_____
_____
_____
_____
_____
_____
_____
_____
_____
_____
_____
_____
_____
_____
_____
_____
_____
_____
_____
_____
_____
_____
_____
_____

Day 27

16. Now the Lord of peace himself give you peace always by all means. The Lord be with you all.
17. The salutation of Paul with mine own hand, which is the token in every epistle: so I write.

2 Thessalonians 3:16–17

Paul's instructions to the people of that time were often straightforward. In this chapter he tells them to withdraw themselves from those who walk disorderly. Paul mentions that he or the brethren that traveled with him didn't eat without working for it. This was an example for those that followed. We can clearly see that Paul is working towards peaceable things of God.

When we are at peace with others our lives will reflect that. He didn't want to take advantage of those people as he was fulfilling his call. When we don't represent God in the right way we cause people to question our motives. Peace is what we should strive for.

This passage simply says the Lord is peace. He wants peace to be the center of all our doings. With all that lies within us we should live peaceably with all men. This may be a different look at peace. Yet the end goal is to have peace in your soul. Let's keep peace as much as possible.

Prayer (speak aloud)

Your Word is our roadmap. You are the God of peace. I strive for peace in every area. Help me, God, when life is being a little stormy. When the waves are knocking me around. Be with me when I'm on display to show forth that peace. I never want to take advantage of others. I need that peace that Paul is talking about. Help me to obey your principles centered around peace. Help me to be the light that others can see their way through different situations. I want to be the peace they need. Many times I'm the only Bible that people will read. Thank You for the revelation of having peace with others will cause peace to flow through my spiritual man as well. Amen.

**Have you ever had a situation where you kept peace and it brought peace to your soul?
I encourage you to read this chapter and get the whole picture that Paul is teaching.**

Day 28

The LORD **is my shepherd; I shall not want.**
Psalm 23:1

Let's spend a few of these reflections in the life of the men in the Bible. King David was a man of war. Fighting and praying seemed to be his moto. Peace was often far from him. So why David? Why this verse? It shouts peace.

This one verse can bring our troubled mind to a place of peace. David knew how to calm the storm within. The book of Psalms is full of peace. This chapter alone has caused the worst storms in my life to cease. Everytime we go through a hard trial this passage will make its way into our heart. It's a metaphor of a shepherd leading his sheep to safety. We know Jesus is known as the true shepherd. Still waters and green grass. A perfect picture of peace.

When we walk through the dark valley we can have peace in our souls. His rod (protection) and staff (guidance) comfort us.

There is no lack in God's pasture. David always found peace in the truth of who God was, we can too.

Prayer (speak aloud)

Dear Lord, You are my shepherd. You are my comfort. Most of all You are my peace. Thank You for leading me through the valleys. You are always right beside me. You will never leave me or forsake me. King David often failed. I often fail as well. Psalm 23 is full of peace. I find myself in every verse. I am a sheep in constant need of saving. I wander too far from safety. I get in the ditch more than I like to admit. My soul gets overwhelmed with all the demands on my life. Often I run on empty. I don't have enough in my cup. That is the fleshy me. Thank You for Psalm 23 and the transparency of King David. Because of these examples I can walk in peace. Amen.

**Can you quote this chapter?
Share your insight about this chapter.
How do you feel about King David?**

Day 29

21. And said, Naked came I out of my mother's womb, and naked shall I return thither: the LORD gave, and the LORD hath taken away; blessed be the name of the LORD. 22. In all this Job sinned not, nor charged God foolishly.

Job 1:21–22

Peace seems to be far from Job. There are 42 chapters in the book of Job. If I was to do a book report I would use chapter 1 and chapter 42. The language in verse 21 lets us know that he trusted God with all his heart. I sense peace between the lines.

Job didn't have the greatest friends. They were of no comfort to him. Don't be so hard on Job's friends though. They were looking from a cultural view. Maybe that's all they knew.

Even Job questioned his very existence. Why was he born? He began to chide with God about his life, he had been sold out to God. What was going on? What Job didn't know was thousands of years later we would read his story and find peace for our own circumstances.

Encourage yourself today through Job's life. In the end he wins. Double for his trouble. Remember Job didn't know the end of his story. That helps me have perfect peace even through my hard seasons.

Prayer (speak aloud)

God of Job, God of David, and God of me, I claim the peace You have created for me. I have seen hard times. I have felt pain and regret. You, oh God, have been my greatest comfort. Thank You for Job. Thank You for all the great men and women in the Bible that went through trials, heartaches, and loss. These soldiers marched on even while the enemy had them surrounded. They found peace in their journey. They didn't always make wise choices, nor did I. Goodness and mercy will follow me all the days of my life. That sounds like peace. Amen.

How many times have you reflected on Job's story to bring peace into your own battle?
What are some of the highlights of the book of Job that you think of when you are needing peace?

_____
_____
_____
_____
_____
_____
_____
_____
_____
_____
_____
_____
_____
_____
_____
_____
_____
_____
_____
_____
_____
_____

Day 30

14. But I trusted in thee, O LORD**: I said, Thou art my God.
15. My times are in thy hand: deliver me from the hand of mine enemies, and from them that persecute me.**

Psalm 31:14–15

If peace had another word in the Bible it would be trust. David could have easily said I have peace in the oh Lord; thou art my God. The book of Psalms is mainly composed of David's writings and his life's journey. It's a book with ups and downs. Defeats and victories. War and peace. The main theme though seems to always point to peace.

Chapter 37 reminds us that the steps of a good man are ordered by the Lord. Delight thyself in the Lord. Rest in the Lord. Commit thy ways unto the Lord. Wait patiently for the Lord. Don't fear. Don't fret. God is a God of peace. He wants us to have peace in homes. Peace on our jobs. Peace in our soul.

Romans 12:18 says, "If it be possible, as much as lieth in you, live peaceably with all men." All means all. With your co-workers. With your in-laws. With your family. Let the peace of God rule in your hearts, to which we are called, and be thankful. Let's find peace in all areas.

Prayer (speak aloud)

I trust You, Lord. I have peace in my soul because of Your goodness. Thank You for ordering my steps. I have peace knowing that my times are in Your hands. I lift my heart to You today knowing that You are in the details of my life. Oh what peace that brings me. It's not always easy to be still and not fret. Thank You God for courage to stand when life is throwing curve balls. Let Your Holy Spirit comfort me. Let the boldness I need rise up at the right time. I put my hope in You and only You. This position that I take in Your Word gives me a peace that is above all the chaos that surrounds me. Peace, peace, wonderful peace. Amen.

Take a few minutes and write out your favorite scriptures in Psalms that speak peace to your soul.

Day 31

7. And the peace of God, which passeth all understanding, shall keep your hearts and minds through Christ Jesus.
8. Finally, brethren, whatsoever things are true, whatsoever things are honest, whatsoever things are just, whatsoever things are pure, whatsoever things are lovely, whatsoever things are of good report; if there be any virtue, and if there be any praise, think on these things.

Philippians 4:7–8

The mind is like a garden, and thoughts are the seeds planted there. You will water those seeds to grow and produce fruit. We must be careful what seeds we allow to take root.

We are bombarded daily with our thoughts. Some good, some bad. No matter how much we try, the bad will still come knocking on our minds. Eight things are listed in verse 8. The word *finally* is simply another word for *intentional*. When we think on the right things, then we can see verse 7 come alive in our life.

The peace of God which passeth all understanding will keep our minds through Christ Jesus. Early in my writing journey I wrote *How to Be Intentional with Your Words*. Whatever we are thinking on will usually come forth as words. Thoughts and Words go hand in hand. They can set you up for victory or cause you to fall into a place of despair. The mind is a battleground. Many times we win or lose in our minds first.

Thank God for peace that will be with us day in and day out. Let's be hopeful, joyful, and peaceful.

Prayer (speak aloud)

I am thankful for Your Word. You were very intentional about what You wanted in the Bible. The scripture teaches me how to be peaceful. I can think on things that are just, pure, lovely. I can praise You in the storms. I can call on Your name and peace will flood my soul. As I'm finishing up this devotional I am encouraged to stay hopeful, joyful, and peaceful. You didn't leave me without a remedy. Thank You for sending Jesus Christ to die on the cross to save my soul from a Devil's hell. I will always seek peace when life gets crazy. Even pursue it. Amen.

What is something you do when your mind gets bombarded with negative thoughts?
I challenge you to do what verse 8 says. Think on the good things.
Journal about some things that bring peace.

Why bees?

My series of Bee Devotionals was birthed out of a deep desire to have a ministry that would encourage, inspire, and pour into somebody else who wants to make a difference. Don't let what others say about you or even your own thinking limit a limitless God. The bumblebee shouldn't be able to fly because of the structure of its body, but it flies anyway. So can you.

Over the next few years, I'm hoping to develop a total of 12 "How to Be…" devotionals to inspire and encourage Christians who want more out of life. My YouTube channel for Bee Ministries offers devotional readings, sermons, heartfelt stories, and inspirational words. My first book, *Life After the Mistake*, is a creative nonfiction story about what it's like to be caught up in the sin of adultery. It's available on Amazon along with the Bee Devotional series and a short ebook I developed called *How to Bee a Writer*.

From the bottom of my heart, thank you for reading my book and taking the time to let God work within you through words. It changed me. And I believe it can change you too.

-Sheila

MORE BOOKS BY SHEILA TEXTOR

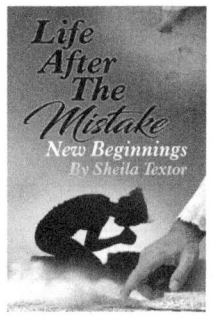

Victory

She is strong. She is vibrant.

She flourishes throughout each new devotional. She flies around the journal pages to keep you focused on your own thoughts for that day. She carries the promises of the word through the daily reflections.
She is my sweet Victory!

She is vibrant, she is positive, she is Victory!

NEED MORE SPACE TO JOURNAL?

NEW RELEASE!

ALL BOOKS AVAILABLE ON AMAZON

Made in the USA
Middletown, DE
15 November 2025

21649210R00080